WORLD LEADERS' FAVOURITE POEMS

A Book of Peace

I would like to thank you all for helping me make this book possible. My thanks go, in particular, to my friend Juliana Hepp.

Mehmet Basci

Parthian
The Old Surgery
Napier Street
Cardigan
SA43 1ED

www.parthianbooks.co.uk

First published in 2008
© the authors 2008
All Rights Reserved

ISBN 978-1-902638-98-0

Compiled by Mehmet Basci

Edited by Lucy Llewellyn

 Project managed by
www.iconau.com

With thanks to Nigel and Jane Evans

Design & typesetting
by Lucy Llewellyn

Printed & bound by Dinefwr Press, Llandybïe, Wales

British Library Cataloguing in Publication Data

A cataloguing record for this book is available
from the British Library.

WORLD LEADERS' FAVOURITE POEMS

A Book of Peace

Compiled by *Mehmet Basci*

PARTHIAN

CONTENTS

We willingly confuse politics with realism even though it is poetry that comes from the domain of dreams, and is therefore from the ideal. There seems to be an incompatibility between action and dreams – politics is deemed the most elevated expression of action, and poetry has the privilege of expressing dreams. However, if we go back to the source, here I mean the Greek, in the translation of the verb 'to do' we find two options: 'poiein' from which we get 'poiesis' (poetry) and 'prattein' which changes to 'praxis', meaning action. In other words, poetry and action are for the Greeks, our first masters in thought, two forms of creative activity.

These words of President Georges Pompidou, read at a Comédie Française poetry evening on 28th April 1969, could well have been written for this collection by Mehmet Basci. It is an original idea to attempt to understand the motivation behind the political actions of heads of state, or government, through their poetic preferences. By declaring their poetic tastes, the men and women who represent states and are confronted with sometimes difficult daily choices show us where they find part of their inspiration. This shows us too the extent to which daily political action finds a source of reflection in texts that express timeless truths.

Rainer Maria Rilke's *The Panther*, Jorge Luis Borges' *Chess* and Fernando Pessoa's *This* show us how three great intellectuals and poets of the 20th century knew how to be not only men of their time, but also universal thinkers. Reflecting on the absolute is the poet's pastime while reacting to the present is the duty of the politician. Reading this collection enables us to appreciate how these two worlds meet. Any political action that is not equally motivated by a quest for the absolute is limited and partial. Any poetical or literary work that is not ingrained in the culture and society of its time is not fully understandable.

Poetry and practice, reflection and action are the tools that we use to work in our profession. The significance of Mehmet Basci's collection is to remind us of this.

Micheline Calmy-Rey
Swiss Federal Councillor for Foreign Affairs

1

We should find joy in the things that our lives have to offer us. Joy both in the wealth of our human experiences, and in the gift of language, which allows us to communicate, and unite, over these shared experiences. Though our history has been littered with times of conflict and pain, peace is a possibility that lies just in front of us, perhaps just one moment away at any given time. We should perpetually seek it out, as naturally and as resolutely as we each seek out warmth in the cold winter.

Tomorrow is yet unwritten. Let us write a world of tolerance, of acceptance, of patience. Let each individual seek out peace, and society will one day find it. Let us respect and protect each other, and remember always to value the frailty, beauty and fleetingness of human life and all that we can create within our lives.

Poetry is a 'mirror to the soul', and I hope that this book might allow us all to reflect on our leaders and our lands, but more importantly, on the things that unite us; our common hopes, fears and pleasures. Like a single drop in a vast ocean, I hope this book may make a small contribution to our realising a shared goal; a happy, healthy and peaceful world.

Mehmet Basci

Bern, 17. September 2003

Herrn
Mehmet Basci
Feldbergstrasse 33
4057 Basel

Sehr geehrter Herr Basci

Mit Schreiben vom 12. August 2003 haben Sie darum gebeten, Ihnen das Lieblingsgedicht von Herrn Bundespräsident Pascal Couchepin zu übermitteln.

In Absprache mit Herrn Couchepin lasse ich Ihnen anbei eine Kopie des Gedichts von *John Donne* "*No man is an island*" zukommen. Ich hoffe, Ihnen damit gedient zu haben.

Mit freundlichen Grüssen

Benno Bättig

Beilage erwähnt

4

Pascal Couchepin

Pascal Couchepin, born on 5th April 1942, is President of the Swiss Confederation for 2008. Previously, he has been Deputy Mayor (1976) and Mayor of Martigny (since 1984).

Devotions upon Emergent Occasions

No man is an island, entire of it self;
Every man is a piece of the Continent, a part of the main;
If a clod be washed away by the sea, Europe is the less,
As well as if a promontory were,
As well as if a manor of thy friends or of thine own were;
Any man's death diminishes me, because I am involved in Mankind;
And therefore never send to know for whom the bell tolls;
It tolls for thee.

John Donne
1572–1631, England

Gordon Brown

James Gordon Brown, born 20th February 1951, in Glasgow, is Prime Minister of the United Kingdom. He took office on 27th June 2007, three days after becoming leader of the Labour Party. He is also the United Kingdom's longest-serving Chancellor since Nicholas Vansittart in the early 19th century.

The Hands of Others

It is the hands of other people
that supply the needs of our bodies,
both in our infancy and beyond.
For each of us lives in and through
an immense movement
of the hands of other people.
The hands of other people lift us from the womb.
The hands of other people grow the food we eat,
weave the clothes we wear and
build the shelters we inhabit.
The hands of other people give pleasure to our bodies
in moments of passion
and aid and comfort in times of affliction and distress.
It is in and through the hands of other people
that the commonwealth of nature is appropriated
and accommodated to the needs and pleasures
of our separate, individual lives, and,
at the end,
it is the hands of other people that lower us into the earth.

James Stockinger
b. 1946, USA

Chandrika Bandaranaike Kumaratunga

Chandrika Bandaranaike Kumaratunga, born on 29th June 1945, was the fifth President, and first female President, of Sri Lanka from November 1994 to November 2005. She was the leader of the Sri Lanka Freedom Party until the end of 2005. Her father, Solomon Bandaranaike was Prime Minister before he was assassinated in 1959, when Chandrika was fourteen. Her mother, Sirimavo Bandaranaike, then became the world's first female Prime Minister in 1960.

Pity the Nation

My friends and my road-fellows, pity the nation
that is full of beliefs and empty of religion.
"Pity the nation that wears a cloth it does not weave...
eats bread it does not harvest...
and drinks a wine that flows not from its own winepress.

"Pity the nation that acclaims the bully as a hero,
and that deems the glittering conqueror bountiful.

"Pity the nation that raises not its voice save when it
walks in a funeral, boasts not except among its ruins,
and will rebel not save when its neck is laid between
the sword and the block.

"Pity the nation whose statesman is a fox, whose
philosopher is a juggler, and whose art is the art of
patching and mimicking.

"Pity the nation that welcomes its new ruler with
trumpetings, and farewells him with hooting, only to
welcome another with trumpeting again.

"Pity the nation divided into fragments, each fragment
deeming itself a nation."

Kahlil Gibran
1883–1931, Lebanon

Stjepan Mesić

Stjepan Mesić was born on 24th December 1934, in Orahovica, Kingdom of Yugoslavia. A Croatian politician, he has been President of the Republic of Croatia since 2000. He had previously held the posts of Prime Minister of Croatia, final President of Socialist Yugoslavia, and President of the Croatian Parliament.

Small Fruit Tree after Rain

Consider the small fruit tree after the rain:
full of trembling raindrops
the enchanted magnificence of its branches
glitters in the sunlight.

Yet when the sun hides, in a moment
the magic vanishes.
It is again, as it was before,
an ordinary, poor little tree.

Dobrisa Cesarić
1902–1980, Croatia

Translated by Jeni Williams & Pavlija Jovic
After the Croation of Dobrisa Cesarić

Ludwig Derangadage Scotty

Ludwig Derangadage Scotty was born on 20th June 1948, in Anabar. He was President of the Republic of Nauru from May to August 2003, and also from June 2004 to December 2007.

Pinnacles Exposed

Scorched, by searing rays of sun, bleached white;
Exposed, to elements of wind and rain, stood firm;
Forgotten, by generations of man and beast, eerily lonely;
Await, fateful destiny for restoration and use, obediently silent;
Forever beckoning to the heaven's universe,
                               through merciful abeyance;
Disturbed, spirits of ancestors long gone, wailing on the breeze;
Groaning, amongst debris of machinery derelict, voices unclear;
Mesmerized, by haunting moonlit shaded, in peaceful bliss;
Carefree, days bygone on forefathers' land, in reminiscence;
Witness, the ultimate destruction of Naoero land, for gains;
Leaving only birds afraid, hunted by man with aid;
To forever linger, undisturbed, until rehabilitation proper.

President Ludwig Scotty
b. 1948, Nauru

Ian Paisley

Ian Richard Kyle Paisley was born on 6th April 1926 in Armagh. As
the leader of the Democratic Unionist Party, he was elected First
Minister of Northern Ireland on 8th May 2007. A veteran politician
and church leader, he is also a prolific author, lecturer and speaker.
His chosen poem was given to him by his father on his ordination to
the Christian ministry.

Words of Remembrance
and Resolve

I must go on:
My hand is put unto the plough;
The wind blows cold; the sluggard leaves the sod unturned;
Nor cares that in the time of harvest he must beg!
But I have seen a Ploughman, spite of wind and snow,
Plough an unbending furrow to the end;
And ceaseless in His toil, break up the fallow ground
And through the mist and murk of unpropitious days
Lay up in store the summer's golden harvest joy
That Ploughman is the Master of my soul;
Therefore, in spite of storm and stress, like Him,
I must go on!

I must fight on:
I have in conscience drawn the sword;
The fight is hard; the armed Ephraimites may flee
And fill the streets of Gath and Askelon with mirth;
But I have seen a Warrior take the field alone,
Unsheath His sword against infernal foes,
And, with undaunted soul, cut through the serried ranks;
And, though forsaken of the men He came to save,
Pour out His blood to win for them the victor's crown.
That Warrior is the Captain of my soul,
And I, though I should stand alone, like Him,
I must fight on!

And I must love:
My heart is longer not my own.

The world allures, and fickle hearts may turn aside,
Nor cares that ashes mark the place of yester's flame;
But I have seen a Lover, spite of scorn and hate,
Love through an agony of blood and tears;
And ceaseless in His love for e'en his enemies,
Lay down His life, forsaken of the earth and sky,
And, rising, win a bride, and ring the marriage bells!
That Lover is the Lover of my soul;
And I, unto the endless end, like Him,
I too must love!

T. T. Shields
1873 – 1955, England

Carlos Diego Mesa Gisbert

Carlos Diego Mesa Gisbert, born on 12th August 1953, is a Bolivian politician, historian and was President of Bolivia from October 2003 until his resignation in June 2005. He is a member of the Bolivian History Academy, and co-wrote (along with his parents, themselves noted scholars and professionals) an exhaustive compendium of Bolivian history from the coming of the Spaniards to the close of the millennium.

The Game of Chess

1.

Seated in their serious corners, the players
Align the slow pieces. The board
Holds them until dawn in its severe
Enclosure, two colours hating each other.

The game magically enforces discipline
Upon its forms: Homeric castle, light-
Footed knight, warring queen, the king
In the rear, his bishop at a slant, pawns advancing.

When the players have gone away,
When time at last consumes them,
The ritual is certainly not over.

It was the Orient that sparked this war
And now the whole earth is its theatre.
As with that other game, this one is forever.

2.

Frail king, slippery bishop, bloody-minded
Queen, single-minded rook, smooth-tongued
Pawn, both the black and the white, seek the path
That finds the other out, armed to the teeth.

What they do not know is that the pointing
Hand of the player is governor of destiny.

Nor do they know what adamantine ways
Bind their will and shape their journey.
The player, however, is also a prisoner
(The saying of Omar's) of yet another
Checkerboard of nights and days.

God moves the player as he the pieces
But what god behind God plots the advent
Of dust and time and dreams and agonies?

Jorge Luis Borges
1899–1986, Argentina

Translated by Kurt Heinzelman
After the Spanish of Jorge Luis Borges

Ilham Heydar oglu Aliyev

Ilham Heydar oglu Aliyev, born on 24th December 1961, in Baku, has been the President of Azerbaijan since 2003. His father, Heydar Aliyev, stepped down due to ill health and appointed Ilham as his party's sole presidential candidate. He also functions as the head of the New Azerbaijan Party.

Azerbaijan

I've walked these mountains again and again,
Passed by the springs bright-eyed as cranes,
And caught the distant plashing strain
Where quiet Araks' waters moved:
Here love and friends I've truly proved.
Men know that you are mine by birth:
My nest, my refuge, and my hearth,
My mother, native land, dear earth!
Sever soul and body? Death but can.
O Azerbaijan, my Azerbaijan!
As mother to me, as child to you –
Such is the bond we ever knew:
I'd come back wherever I flew,
For you are my people, you – my nest,
My native birthplace ever blest.

When I'm away, your face unseen,
When times and forces intervene,
My hair is touched with silver sheen –
For months and years press age on me:
My land, don't blame your absentee.
Your mountain crests are topped with snow,
And cloud – a shawl of fleecy flow,
Your past is greater than we know.
Your age from everyone obscured,
And none may guess what you've endured.
Evil tongues spread defamation –
You lived through years of dark privation.
Still, generation to generation

Your fame lives on: a benison
To happy daughter, happy son.

Khazar the sea you border on
Where floats the legendary swan...
My day-dreams sweep me swiftly on
To Mugan Lowland, on to Miell:
A long-life road-half-done, I feel.
The mountain ranges, valley sweep,
Gladden the heart till it could weep...
Glimpse of startled fawn and chamois leap –
How much beauty on which to gazei-
Pastures cool and steppes ablaze.
Cross the mountains, over steppe-land,
Or through Astar, Lenkoran –
From African and Indian strand
Birds fly to visit, with us pause,
Freed from oppressive grasping claws.

It's here the yellow lemons grow,
The heavy branches weighting low.
Up in the mountains, white the snow
And deep from winter's opulence:
Since Creation – a true defense.
Lenkoran is a dazzle of flowers,
Refreshed by the springtime showers,
Clustering on beds and bowers,
My motherland's delightful daughter,
Bordered on by Khazar's water.
The golden wheat we grow – our bread,
Our cotton-wealth of snowy heads;
Squeeze the juice from grapes wine-red –

Before you breakfast, drain a cup
And feel your spirit surging up,

In Khazakh mount, and give free rein,
Lean well over the horse's mane,
A sweating gallop then maintain:
On reaching mountain pastures high,
Look down on Goy-Gyol-mirrored sky.
Across your valleys long I stare,
On clear days full of lucent air;
My spirit broods on faces fair,
Thirsting for poetic tongue –
Creating verses makes me young.
A day that's free, a man that's free,
A spring like this invites a spree,
Seek out the shade of a plane tree
To spread a rug that's rainbow-spun –
And hail the country of the Sun!

Through Karabakh my spirit fares,
Wings over mountain here, now there;
From far away down the twilit all –
Drifts the song – of Khan of Shusha –
Famed through all Caucasus and Russia –
Beautiful birth land! Your meaning deep,
Cradle of Beauty that never sleeps,
Where songs of bard, inspired, sweep.
The sun's embrace – your counterpart,
O land of poetry and art.

Spirit immortal, works immortal;
Nazimi, Fisuli – are immortal!

On pen and paper, open the portals
Of your soul, record the flow:
The word once writ – through time will go.

Look at the sea near our Baku:
Its shore a bright-lit avenue,
The derricks roaring right in view;
The thunder where the steppe-land swales –
To light the mountains and the vales.
The cool wind is a merry tease,
We bare our chests to the off-shore breeze.
Our heart, Baku on Caspian seas –
Its light – our very strength adorning:
Our Morning Star – clear eye of morning.

Beautiful birth land! I was born
Together with freedom's dawn
Which crimson banners did adorn –
Life seemed one endless, joyous feast;
Gay songs and laughter never ceased.
Dear country – gate of the Ancient East.

Samad Vurgun
1906–1956, Azerbaijan

Translated by Gladys Evans
After the original Azeri of Samad Vurgun

Matti Vanhanen

Matti Vanhanen, was born on 4th November 1955, in Jyväskylä. He was a journalist before becoming a politician. He became Prime Minister of Finland in June 2003. His favourite poem is taken from the novel *Seven Brothers*.

The Squirrel

Snug the squirrel lies
In his mossy lair
Where no tooth of Frost
Has ever reached.
From his lofty cell
He surveys all things
With their strife below
As a peace-flag swings
High on the pine.

In the cradle-fort
What a joy to rest
Rocking in the sweet
Spruce's mother-breast
To Forestland's music!
At a small window
The bobtail dozes
And the birds sing him
When the day closes
To Dreamland's gold.

Aleksis Kivi
1834–1872, Finland

A.P.J. Abdul Kalam

A.P.J. Abdul Kalam, born 15th October 1931, in Rameshwaram, was the eleventh President of India, serving from 2002 to 2007. Kalam is a distinguished scientist and has received honorary doctorates from about thirty universities. He observes strict personal discipline, including vegetarianism, teetotalism and celibacy.

The Life Tree

Oh, my human race,
How, we were born,
In the Universe of near infinity,
Are we alone?

I was seeking answer for the great
Question of creation, weighing heavy
My mind as I am in seventieth orbit
Around sun, my little habitat, the star
Where my race living, lived billions of years
And will live billions of years, till the sun shines.
This is the millennium question of humanity,
And sought the help of our creator.

On the eventful day, I was flying
The earth below me, the human habitat
Vanished in the white river of cloud,
Silent, turbulent free everywhere the divine
Splendour reflecting.
On the above, the full moon with its magnificent might,
My heart melted, my friend co-passenger
Vidyasagar joined in the heavenly display.
The beauty entered into our soul
And blossomed happiness into our mind and body.
We the humanity bowed to the heavenly answer,
We are not alone, billion of billion lives
Of various forms spring in the planets of
Galaxy after galaxies.
Then the dawn of divine message.

There was the divine echo in the full moon night
From my creator.
Shaken, bewildered and wondered
The echo engulfed me and my race
"You, the human race is the best of my creation
You will live and live.
You give and give till you are united,
In human happiness and pain.
My bliss will be born in you
Love is continuum.
That is the mission of humanity,
You will see every day in Life Tree
You learn and learn
My best of creations."
Beautiful morning it was,
Sun radiating, driving away the clouds
Parrots and Kokilas were at their musical flight
We the yellow heaven group entered
Flower garden of Asiad
Roses were in their splendour
Radiating beauty in White and Crimson
Bowing to the dawn of sun
We walked and walked, our feet on the green
Meadow giving velvet touch,
Children somewhere ringing in unison in their innocence
Peacocks in the background giving beautiful display.

There was a majestic scene of Life Tree
Cluster of tall and straight Nag phalli grove
Undaunted to the sun rays direction
Multi layered, each flower plant bubbling with life,
We approached very close to the happy plants

Astonished to see the nature's wonder.
Bottom layers have shed the flower all around the sand
Whereas mid layer flower blossomed
In number to the magnificence
Perfume radiating, beauty all around
Honey bees filling the flower bed, mutual love flowing
Intoxicated with the scene, we looked at the top layer
Ring of the buds about to blossom
And new layers at their birth.

Again the great divine echo enters all around us
"Flowers blossom, radiate beauty and spread perfume
And give honey. On the eve of life
Flowers silently fall to the earth, they belong.
Oh my creation this is mission of human life
You are born, live life of giving
And bond the human life
Your mission is the Life Tree.
My blessings to you my creation."

Oh my human race
Let's sing the song of creation.

A.P.J. Abdul Kalam
b. 1931, India

Sam Nujoma

Samuel Daniel Shafiishuna Nujoma, born on 12th May 1929, was the first President of Namibia. He was inaugurated in 1990 and subsequently re-elected in 1994 and 1999, serving until 2005. He was also President of the South-West Africa People's Organisation (SWAPO) from its founding in 1960 until 2007.

Comrade Sam Nujoma

His easily recognizable bearded face
Appeared on many a newspaper page
He certainly oozed enviable charisma
As he rubbed shoulders in the diplomatic arena
For several Parties struggled for media space
To explain to friendly governments their case
Comrade Sam Nujoma knew colonialism's bitter taste

His easily recognizable bearded face
Known to thousands of children in our settlement
Because it is for their daily nourishment
That he attended many a conference in any case
To feed exiled little mouths on his return to base
With a bag full of maize meal as part of his luggage
He knew how to vigorously present our case

His easily recognizable bearded face
Brought comfort to wounded soldiers
As we off-loaded medicine in Lubango
Sent from afar as urgently needed cargo
To cure soldiers from the battle-field
As trained hands worked with maximum speed
He saluted those that heroically sacrificed

His easily recognizable bearded face
Appealed to thousands of patriotic Namibians
As he urged us to fight with aid from Tanzanians
And political asylum granted by the selfless Zambians

We joined forces with neighbouring free Angola
As we were reinforced by internationalist Cuba
Comrade Nujoma knew he was fighting for Africa

His easily recognizable bearded face
Appeared on many a television screen
As he debated our thorny question with tact
To liberate our mineral-rich country intact
He influenced many a decision-maker in fact
For the United Nations to seriously consider
General elections with the world body as supervisor.

Mvula ya Nangolo
b. 1943, Namibia

Néstor Kirchner

Néstor Kirchner, born on 25th February 1950, was President of Argentina from May 2003 to December 2007. A Justicialist with leftist leanings, Kirchner was previously governor of the province of Santa Cruz.

The Just

A man who cultivates a garden, the way Voltaire wanted.
One who is grateful there is music in the world.
Who delights in knowing where words come from.
Two workmen who, in a café in the South, play chess silently.
The potter who deliberates over form and colour.
The typesetter who lays out this page well but still is not pleased
A woman and a man reading the last tercets of a certain canto.
One who strokes a sleeping animal.
Who justifies, or wishes to, a wrong done to him.
Who is grateful for Stevenson,
Who prefers others to be right.
These are the people who, ignored, are saving the world.

Jorge Luis Borges
1899–1986, Argentina

Translated by Kurt Heinzelman
After the Spanish of Jorge Luis Borges

Guy Verhofstadt

Guy Maurice Marie Louise Verhofstadt, born on 11th April 1953, in Dendermonde, has been Prime Minister of Belgium since 1999. He is the author of several books.

This

They say I pretend or lie
All I write. No such thing.
It simply is that I
Feel by imagining.
I don't use the heart-string.

All that I dream or lose,
That falls short or dies on me.
Is like a terrace which looks
On another thing beyond.
It's that thing leads me on.

And so I write in the middle
Of things not next one's feet,
Free from my own muddle,
Concerned for what is not.
Feel? Let the reader feel!

Fernando Pessoa
1888–1935, Portugal

Translated by Jonathon Griffin
After the Portuguese of Fernando Pessoa

Gerry Adams

Gerard Adams MP, born on 6th October 1948, in West Belfast, is an Irish Republican politician and abstentionist Member for Belfast West of the Westminister Parliament. Adams is a spokesman for the Irish Republican Movement which encompasses Sinn Féin, of which he is President, and the Provisional Irish Republican Army. Adams is widely regarded as having played a pivotal role in getting the IRA to give up its armed campaign against the UK in return for devolved government for Northern Ireland.

The Lake Isle of Innisfree

I will arise and go now, and go to Innisfree,
And a small cabin build there, of clay and wattles made:
Nine bean-rows will I have there, a hive for the honeybee,
And live alone in the bee-loud glade.

And I shall have some peace there, for peace comes dropping slow,
Dropping from the veils of the morning to where the cricket sings;
There midnight's all a glimmer, and noon a purple glow,
And evening full of the linnet's wings.

I will arise and go now, for always night and day
I hear lake water lapping with low sounds by the shore;
While I stand on the roadway, or on the pavements grey,
I hear it in the deep heart's core.

William Butler Yeats
1865–1939, Ireland

Gerhard Fritz Kurt Schröder

Gerhard Fritz Kurt Schröder was born on 7th April 1944, in Mossenberg. He was Chancellor of Germany from 1998 to 2005. He spoke out strongly against the war on Iraq, refusing any military assistance in that enterprise, causing political friction between the USA and Germany.

Jean-Claude Juncker

Jean-Claude Juncker, born on 9th December 1954, in Redange, is a Luxembourgian politician. He is the leader of the Christian Social People's Party and Prime Minister of Luxembourg. He has also held the position of Minister for Finances since 1989.

The Panther

His gaze, going past those bars, has got so misted
with tiredness, it can take in nothing more.
He feels as though a thousand bars existed,
and no more world beyond them than before.

Those supply powerful paddings, turning there
in tiniest of circles, well might be
the dance of forces round a centre where
some mighty will stands paralytically.

Just now and then the pupils' noiseless shutter
is lifted. – Then an image will indart,
down through the limbs' intensive stillness flutter,
and end its being in the heart.

Rainer Maria Rilke
1875–1926, Austria

Translated by William Leishman
After the German of Rainer Maria Rilke

José María Aznar López

José María Aznar López, born on 25th February 1953, in Madrid, served as the President of the Government of Spain (Prime Minister) from 1996 to 2004.

If

If you can keep your head when all about you
Are losing theirs and blaming it on you,
If you can trust yourself when all men doubt you
But make allowance for their doubting too,
If you can wait and not be tired by waiting,
Or being lied about, don't deal in lies,
Or being hated, don't give way to hating,
And yet don't look too good, nor talk too wise:
If you can dream – and not make dreams your master,
If you can think – and not make thoughts your aim;
If you can meet with Triumph and Disaster
And treat those two impostors just the same;
If you can bear to hear the truth you've spoken
Twisted by knaves to make a trap for fools,
Or watch the things you gave your life to, broken,
And stoop and build 'em up with worn-out tools:

If you can make one heap of all your winnings
And risk it all on one turn of pitch-and-toss,
And lose, and start again at your beginnings
And never breathe a word about your loss;
If you can force your heart and nerve and sinew
To serve your turn long after they are gone,
And so hold on when there is nothing in you
Except the Will which says to them: "Hold on!"
If you can talk with crowds and keep your virtue,
Or walk with kings – nor lose the common touch,
If neither foes nor loving friends can hurt you;
If all men count with you, but none too much,

If you can fill the unforgiving minute
With sixty seconds' worth of distance run,
Yours is the Earth and everything that's in it,
And – which is more – you'll be a Man, my son!

Rudyard Kipling
1865–1936, England

Abdul Hamid Pawanteh

H.E. Tan Sri Dato' Seri Abdul Hamid Pawanteh is the President of the Senate (*Dewan Negara*) of the Parliament of Malaysia.

Ode

Intimations of Immortality from Recollections of Early Childhood

There was a time when meadow, grove, and stream,
The earth, and every common sight,
      To me did seem
      Apparelled in celestial light,
The glory and the freshness of a dream.
It is not now as it hath been of yore; –
      Turn wheresoe'er I may,
        By night or day,
The things which I have seen I now can see no more.

      The Rainbow comes and goes,
      And lovely is the Rose;
      The Moon doth with delight
Look round her when the heavens are bare;
      Waters on a starry night
      Are beautiful and fair;
  The sunshine is a glorious birth;
  But yet I know, where'er I go.
That there hath passed away a glory from the earth.

Now, while the birds thus sing a joyous song,
  And while the young lambs bound
      As to the tabor's sound,
To me alone there came a thought of grief:
A timely utterance gave that thought relief,
      And I again am strong:

The cataracts blow their trumpets from the steep;
No more shall grief of mine the season wrong;
I hear the Echoes through the mountains throng,
The winds come to me from the fields of sleep,
   And all the earth is gay;
    Land and sea
  Give themselves up to jollity,
   And with the heart of May
  Doth every Beast keep holiday;
   Thou Child of Joy,
Shout round me, let me hear thy shouts, thou happy
    Shepherd-Boy!

Ye blessed Creatures, I have heard the call
 Ye to each other make; I see
The heavens laugh with you in your jubilee;
 My heart is at your festival,
  My head hath its coronal,
The fulness of your bliss, I feel – I feel it all.
   Oh evil day! if I were sullen
   While Earth herself is adorning,
    This sweet May-morning,
   And the Children are pulling
    On every side,
   In a thousand valleys far and wide,
   Fresh flowers; while the sun shines warm,
And the Babe leaps up on his Mother's arm: –
  I hear, I hear, with joy I hear!
  – But there's a Tree, of many, one,
A single Field which I have looked upon,
Both of them speak of something that is gone:
   The Pansy at my feet
   Doth the same tale repeat:

Whither is fled the visionary gleam?
Where is it now, the glory and the dream?

Our birth is but a sleep and a forgetting:
The Soul that rises with us, our life's Star,
        Hath had elsewhere its setting,
            And cometh from afar:
        Not in entire forgetfulness,
        And not in utter nakedness,
But trailing clouds of glory do we come
        From God, who is our home:
Heaven lies about us in our infancy!
Shades of the prison-house begin to close
        Upon the growing Boy,
But he beholds the light, and whence it flows,
        He sees it in his joy;
The Youth, who daily farther from the east
        Must travel, still is Nature's Priest,
        And by the vision splendid
        Is on his way attended;
At length the Man perceives it die away,
And fade into the light of common day.

Earth fills her lap with pleasures of her own;
Yearnings she hath in her own natural kind,
And, even with something of a Mother's mind,
        And no unworthy aim,
        The homely Nurse doth all she can
To make her Foster-child, her Inmate Man,
        Forget the glories he hath known,
And that imperial palace whence he came.

Behold the Child among his new-born blisses,
A six years' Darling of a pigmy size!
See, where mid work of his own hand he lies,
Fretted by sallies of his mother's kisses,
With light upon him from his father's eyes!
See, at his feet, some little plan or chart,
Some fragment from his dream of human life,
Shaped by himself with newly-learned art;
       A wedding or a festival,
       A mourning or a funeral;
         And this hath now his heart,
         And unto this he frames his song:
          Then will he fit his tongue
To dialogues of business, love, or strife;
        But it will not be long
        Ere this be thrown aside,
        And with new joy and pride
The little Actor cons another part;
Filling from time to time his "humorous stage"
With all the Persons, down to palsied Age,
That Life brings with her in her equipage;
       As if his whole vocation
       Were endless imitation.

Thou, whose exterior semblance doth belie
       Thy Soul's immensity;
Thou best Philosopher, who yet dost keep
Thy heritage, thou Eye among the blind,
That, deaf and silent, read'st the eternal deep,
Haunted for ever by the eternal mind, –
       Mighty Prophet! Seer blest!
       On whom those truths do rest,
Which we are toiling all our lives to find,

In darkness lost, the darkness of the grave;
Thou, over whom thy Immortality
Broods like the Day, a Master o'er a slave,
A Presence which is not to be put by;
      To whom the grave
Is but a lonely bed without the sense or sight
    Of day or the warm light,
A place of thought where we in waiting lie;
Thou little Child, yet glorious in the might
Of heaven-born freedom on thy being's height,
Why with such earnest pains dost thou provoke
The years to bring the inevitable yoke,
Thus blindly with thy blessedness at strife?
Full soon thy Soul shall have her earthly freight,
And custom lie upon thee with a weight,
Heavy as frost, and deep almost as life!

      O joy! that in our embers
      Is something that doth live,
      That nature yet remembers
      What was so fugitive!
The thought of our past years in me doth breed
Perpetual benedictions not indeed
For that which is most worthy to be blest; –
Delight and liberty, the simple creed
Of Childhood, whether busy or at rest,
With new-fledged hope still fluttering in his breast: –
      Not for these I raise
      The song of thanks and praise;
      But for those obstinate questionings
      Of sense and outward things,
      Fallings from us, vanishings;
      Blank misgivings of a Creature

Moving about in worlds not realized,
High instincts before which our mortal Nature
Did tremble like a guilty Thing surprised:
      But for those first affections,
      Those shadowy recollections,
         Which, be they what they may,
Are yet the fountain-light of all our day,
Are yet a master-light of all our seeing;
      Uphold us, cherish, and have power to make
Our noisy years seem moments in the being
Of the eternal Silence: truths that wake,
         To perish never:
Which neither listlessness, nor mad endeavour,
         Nor Man nor Boy,
Nor all that is at enmity with joy,
Can utterly abolish or destroy!
      Hence in a season of calm weather
      Though inland far we be,
Our Souls have sight of that immortal sea
         Which brought us hither,
         Can in a moment travel thither,
And see the Children sport upon the shore,
And hear the mighty waters rolling evermore.

Then sing, ye Birds, sing, sing a joyous song!
         And let the young Lambs bound
         As to the tabor's sound!
We in thought will join your throng,
         Ye that pipe and ye that play,
         Ye that through your hearts to-day
         Feel the gladness of the May!
What though the radiance which was once so bright
Be now for ever taken from my sight,

Though nothing can bring back the hour
Of splendour in the grass, of glory in the flower;
We will grieve not, rather find
Strength in what remains behind;
In the primal sympathy
Which having been must ever be;
In the soothing thoughts that spring
Out of human suffering;
In the faith that looks through death,
In years that bring the philosophic mind.

And O, ye Fountains, Meadows, Hills, and Groves,
Forebode not any severing of our loves!
Yet in my heart of hearts I feel your might;
I only have relinquished one delight
To live beneath your more habitual sway.
I love the Brooks which down their channels fret,
Even more than when I tripped lightly as they;
The innocent brightness of a new-born Day
Is lovely yet;
The Clouds that gather round the setting sun
Do take a sober colouring from an eye
That hath kept watch o'er man's mortality;
Another race hath been, and other palms are won.
Thanks to the human heart by which we live,
Thanks to its tenderness, its joys, and fears,
To me the meanest flower that blows can give
Thoughts that do often lie too deep for tears.

William Wordsworth
1770–1850, England

Tony Blair

Anthony Charles Lynton Blair, born on 6th May 1953, in Edinburgh, served as Prime Minister of the United Kingdom from 1997 to 2007. Re-elected in 1997, 2001, and 2005, Blair was the Labour Party's longest-serving Prime Minister, the only person to lead the party to three consecutive general election victories.

The Soldier

If I should die, think only this of me:
That there's some corner of a foreign field
That is for ever England. There shall be
In that rich earth a richer dust concealed;
A dust whom England bore, shaped, made aware,
Gave, once, her flowers to love, her ways to roam,
A body of England's, breathing English air,
Washed by the rivers, blest by suns of home.

And think, this heart, all evil shed away,
A pulse in the eternal mind, no less
Give somewhere back the thoughts by England given;
Her sights and sounds; dreams happy as her day;
And laughter, learnt of friends; and gentleness,
In hearts at peace, under an English heaven.

Rupert Brooke
1887–1915, England

Vicente Fox

Vicente Fox Quesada, born on 2nd July 1942, in Mexico City, was the President of Mexico from 2000 to 2006. Fox secured his presidential candidacy representing the Alliance for Change, a political coalition formed by the National Action Party and the Ecological Green Party of Mexico. He is currently Co-President (with Pier Ferdinando Casini) of the Centrist Democratic International, an international organization of Christian Democratic political parties.

Sweet Land

INTROIT

I who have sung only the exquisite
score of personal decorum,
today, at center stage, raise my voice
in the manner of a tenor's imitations
of the bass's deep-throated tones
to carve an ode from an epic poem.

I shall navigate through civil waves
with weightless oars, like that
patriot of yore who, with only a rifle,
rowed across the English Channel.

In a muted epic I shall tell that
our land is diamantine, impeccable.

Sweet Land: let me engulf you
in the deepest music of the jungle,
music that molded my expression,
sounds of the rhythmic cadences of axes,
young girls' cries and laughter,
and birds of the carpenter profession.

ACT ONE

Patria: your surface is the gold of maize,

below, the palace of gold medallion kings,
your sky is filled with the heron's flight
and green lightning of parrots' wings.

God-the-Child deeded you a stable,
lust for oil was the gift of the devil.

Above your Capital the hours soar,
hollow-eyed and rouged, in a coach-and-four,
while in your provinces the hours
roll like centavos from insomniac
clocks with fan-tail dove patrols.

Patria: your maimed terrain
is clothed in beads and bright percale.

Sweet Land: your house is still
so vast that the train rolling by seems
only a diminutive Christmas toy.

And in the tumult of the stations,
your brown-skinned face imparts
that immensity to every heart.

Who, on a dark and ominous night
has not, before he knew wrong, held
tight his sweetheart's arm to watch
the splendor of a fireworks display?

Patria: in your tropical abundance
you shimmer with the dolphin's iridescence;
the soul, an aerialist hummingbird,

plights its troth with your golden hair,
and, as offering to your tobacco braids,
my lively race of jarabe dancers
bring their honeyed maguey waters.

Your soil rings of silver, and in your hand
even poverty's piggy-bank rattles a tune,
and in early mornings across the land,
through streets like mirrors, spread
the blessed aromas of fresh-baked bread.

When we are born, you give us notes,
and compotes worthy of Paradise,
then, Sweet Land, your whole being,
all the bounty of earth and air.

To the sad and the joyful you say sí,
that on your loving tongue they savor
your tangy flavor of sesame.

When it thunders, your nuptial sky
fills us with frenzy and delight.
Thunderous clouds, that drench us
with madness, madden the mountain,
mend the lunatic, woo the woman,
raise the dead, demand the Viaticum,
and then, finally, fling God's lumber
across tilled fields shaken with thunder.

Thunderous storm: I hear in your groans
the rattling of coupled skeletons,
I hear the past and what is to come,

I hear the present with its coconut drum.
And in the sound of your coming and going
I hear life's roulette wheel, spinning, spinning...

INTERMISSION
(Cuauhtemoc)

Forever-young grandfather, hear my praise
for the only hero worthy of art.
Anachronistic, farcical,
the rose bows to your nopal;
you magnetize the Spaniard's language
the spout from which flow Catholic prayers
to fill the triumphant zócalo where
the soles of your feet were scorched to ash.

Unlike Caesar, no patrician flush
suffused your face during your pain;
today, your unwreathed head appears,
hemispherically, on a coin.

A spiritual coin upon which is etched
all you suffered: the hollowed-out pirogue
of your capture, the chaos of your creatures,
the sobbing of your mythologies,
the swimming idols, and the Malinche,
but most to bewail is your having been severed
from the curved breast of the empress
as from the breast of a quail.

SECOND ACT

Suave Patria, this is your omen:
the river of virtues of your women.
Your daughters move like sylphs, or,
distilling an invisible alcohol,
webbed in the netting of your sun,
file by like graceful demijohns.

Patria, I love you not as myth
but for the communion of your truth,
as I love the child peering over the rail,
in a blouse buttoned up to her eartips
and skirt to her ankle of fine percale.

Impervious to dishonor, you flower.
I shall believe in you as long as
at the dawn hour one Mexican woman
carries home dough in her shawl,
and from the oven of its inauguration
the aroma spreads across the nation.

Like a Queen of Hearts, Patria, tapping
a vein of silver, you live miraculously,
for the day, like the national lottery.

Your image is the Palacio Nacional,
the same grandeur, and the identical
stature of a boy and a thimble.

In the face of hunger and mortar, Felipe de Jesús,
saint and martyr, will give you a fig.

Suave Patria, gentle vendor of chía,
I want to bear you away in the dark of Lent,
riding a fiery stallion, disturbing
the peace, and dodging shots from police.

Patria, your heart will always have room
for the bird a youngster tenderly
entombs in an empty spool box;
yes, in you our young hide, weeping,
the dried-apple cadavers
of birds that speak our own tongue.

If I am stifling in your July, send me
from the orchard of your hair the cool air
that brings shawls and dripping clay pitchers;
then, if I shiver, let me draw warmth
from your plump rum-punch lips
and your blue-incense breath.

Before your blessed-palm draped balcony
I pass with heavy heart, knowing
you tremble on this Palm Sunday.

Your spirit and style are dying out,
like the vanishing goddess of song
in a country fair – indomitable bosom
challenging straining bodice-
who evoked lust along with life's rhythm.

Patria, I give the key to happiness:
be faithful forever to your likeness:
fifty repeats of the Ave are carved

on the beads of the rosary, and it is
more fortunate than you, Patria suave.

Be constant, be true, your glory
your eyes of abandon and thirsting voice;
tri-color sash across misty breasts,
and an open air throne like a resonant timbrel:
allegory's straw cart!

Ramón López Velarde
1888–1921, Mexico

Translated by Margaret Sayers Pedan
After the Spanish of Ramón López Velarde

Hans Göran Persson

Hans Göran Persson was born on 20th January 1949, in Vingåker in Södermanland. He was the thirty-first Prime Minister of Sweden (1996–2006). He was the leader of the Swedish Social Democratic Party and a member of the Riksdag. He is a member of Swedish Association of Christian Social Democrats.

The Path on which
You Are Walking Alone

The lonely man is the weakest one.
Not because he is alone but because
He is denying what he is carrying
within himself.

Our soul, getting deeper, is the broad
river of life.

The path on which you are walking alone,
is leading away from yourself.

Pär Lagerkvist
1891–1974, Sweden

Rhodri Morgan

Hywel Rhodri Morgan was born 29th September 1939 in Cardiff. He is a Welsh Labour politician and represents Cardiff West at the National Assembly. He is the First Minister of Wales.

Pwllderi

Up on the mountain's where I live
With the little streams and the air above
I can ape the moor birds' forlorn cries –
The nightjar, corncrake, lark and snipe –
But I couldn't puff out a panegyric
Or weave a college-standard lyric
And I'm not beset by gorgeous babes
Turning me hot and cold in waves
And it's things like these make me quite sure
The muse never darkened my study door;
Cause the schoolmaster's always giving out
They're what being a poet's all about

Yesterday, sitting above Pwllderi,
Where eagles lived once, and bears, and bogeys
I thought, those street-smart people living down there
Have no idea it's so wild up here
The shop-counter poof with his tweeds so fancy
Couldn't keep his footing above Pwllderi
You stand up high above this dungeon
Looking down on a bottomless cauldron
Boiling between the greyish crags
Like churnsful of milk or foaming suds.
Just thinking of it this very minute
Sends a shudder through my heart.

This time of year it's dressed up nice
The gorse all yellow and the thorns all white

And the bluebells growing in sky-blue drifts
On the greeny slopes leading to the cliffs
Where the heather lies on the rock in sheaves
You'd swear that someone had fired the hills.
Like a cheeky angel, the summer's been by
With a cruckful of ribbons and frippery,
He's the only one would be fool enough
To waste his wealth on this patch of rough
Chuckling to send the gorse on the edge
To spendthrift its fool's gold over the ledge
A miser would sicken, might fall and drown
To see its sovereigns raining down.

You'll find a little patch of beach
How big would it be? Say two hundred feet.
Yes, there's sand there, but not a lot:
A crescent moon-shape of a spot.
Here you'll see the heron, too,
Plunging his beak in a little pool
Then stalking off on his lordly stilts
For all the world like a toff in silks;
And yet I never saw a man
Leave his footprint on that strand
Though they do say that famous wrecker
Would sometimes venture down – Dai Beca –
He must have had feet as sure as a billy –
Or a private path through the earth's own belly.
If I ever saw anyone in Pwllderi
I'd run home fast as my feet could take me.

And there's thousands of different birds all over –
Seagulls, and hawks, and golden plover

And the rocks so humongously big and stout
And that ugly great point where they roost about
You could swear that it's clouds of tiny flies
Lazily circling something that's died
And you'd almost say, from your airy eyrie,
That shining gull was a butterfly.

And lord above, what a commotion!
Like howling dogs or hell in motion
Crying and whistling, a thousand ravings
Reverberating through all those caverns
I'll never forget that night of dread –
The sailor on the rock, half-dead
Calling, calling: not a soul nearby
And only seagulls to hear his cry
While those hawks, like devils in disguise
Waited for light to leave his eyes.
It's things like these that come to mind
Above Pwllderi, in summertime.

There's only one house around these parts
An old barn of a place, but what a heart!
Tucked into Garn Fowr, Dolgar by name
Its welcome warm and its tea well-famed
Or a bowlful of cawl, you can't beat that,
Full of leeks and potatoes and starred with fat
The pot on its tripod boiling full force,
Fuelled by faggots of blazing gorse
A ladle brim-full, and twice, and thrice
Finer by far than any lobscouse
And a wooden spoon to scrape your bowl
And a hunk of cheese from a huge great wheel.

You can park yourself on an oaken settle
And listen to the shepherd's tale
He won't talk much of the knock he got
Rescuing a lamb from a perilous spot;
Far less admit it took rope and chain
To pull him up safe to the top again;
But with a catch in his voice, he might touch on
What sent him down through rocks and thorns;
Not the animal's price in market sum
But its cry as it bleated for someone to come;
And he'll talk a while of another Man
Who gave his life to save his lambs;
And these are the things that come to mind
Above Pwllderi in the summertime.

Dewi Emrys
1881–1952, Wales

Translated by Elin ap Hywel
After the Welsh of Dewi Emrys

Ariel Sharon

Ariel Sharon, born Ariel Scheinermann on 27th February 1928, is a former Israeli Prime Minister (from March 2001 until April 2006) and military leader whose political career was ended by a massive stroke he suffered in early 2006.

We Are Both
from the Same Village

We are both from the same village,
the same height, the same forelock,
the same clipped speech – what is there to say
for we are from the same village.

We are from the same village,
we walked through the high grass of the fields
and in the evening returned to the village square –
for we are from the same village.

Chorus: And on Friday evening,
         when a soft breeze passes through
         the black tree tops
         I remember you.

In the orange groves
and among the avenues of trees
we always loved the same girls;
but in the end we said – it doesn't matter –
it all stays in the village.

We ran away to the same places.
We went to the same wars.
We crawled among the thorns and brambles
but we returned together to the village.

I remember, in the battle that did not end,

how I suddenly saw how you were broken.
And when the dawn rose among the hills
I brought you back to the village.

You see – we are here in the village –
almost everything has remained almost the same.
I pass through the green fields and you lie
on the other side of the fence.
For we are both from the same village.

Naomi Shemer
1930–2004, Israel

Anders Fogh Rasmussen

Anders Fogh Rasmussen was born on 26th January 1953, in Ginnerup, Jutland. He is the current Prime Minister of Denmark, at a time of a huge reform of the structure of government in Denmark. Rasmussen received the most 'personal votes' ever of any politician in the *Folketing* (Denmark's Parliament).

Living in the Moment

To live in the moment's a well-worn routine
that most of the world has perfected;
for some, it's the moment that's already been,
for others, the one that's expected.

Yet no sort of magic can kindle anew
a past that is over forever,
nor summon the future before it is due:
our moment is now – or it's never.

So brief is the moment in which we may live,
and future or past it isn't.
Whoever would know of what life hast to give
must gratefully welcome the present.

Piet Hein
1905–1996, Denmark